Facts and ARTEFACTS

ANCIENT EGYPT

Anita Croy

W
FRANKLIN WATTS
LONDON•SYDNEY

Published in Great Britain in 2018 by
The Watts Publishing Group

Copyright © 2018 Brown Bear Books Ltd

For Brown Bear Books Ltd:
Managing Editor: Tim Cooke
Children's Publisher: Anne O'Daly
Editorial Director: Lindsey Lowe
Design Manager: Keith Davis
Designer and Illustrator: Supriya Sahai
Picture Manager: Sophie Mortimer

Concept development: Square and Circus/
Brown Bear Books Ltd

ISBN: 978 1 4451 6185 3

Printed in Malaysia

Franklin Watts
An imprint of
Hachette Children's Group
Part of the Watts Publishing Group
Carmelite House
50 Victoria Embankment
London EC4Y 0DZ

An Hachette UK company
www.hachette.co.uk
www.franklinwatts.co.uk

FSC
www.fsc.org
MIX
Paper from
responsible sources
FSC® C137506

Picture credits
Front Cover: Public Domain: top, Carsten Frenzi,
bottom; Shutterstock: Dan Breckwoldt main.
Interior: Alamy: Heritage Image Partnership/CM
Dixon, 10–11; Dreamstime: Mahdy Mahmod, 7b,
Perseomedusa, 23b; istockphoto: jsanchez_bcn,
7t, Terry Lawrence, 9b, 24–25, Leamus, 5, Lindrik,
13b, redtea, 9t, Sculples, 13t, uchar, 14bl; Public
Domain: 25br, Carsten Frenzi, 11b, Louis le Grand,
25t, Hans Hillewaert, 21tr, Oxford Encyclopedia
of Ancent Egypt, 23t, Keith Schengili-Roberts, 19,
Print Collector/Ancient History Images, 17tl,
Walters Art Museum, 15br; Shutterstock: 17br,
Arijo, 11t, BasPosot, 26, Anton Ivanov, 18–19,
matrioshka, 14–15, meunierd, 6–7, Pecold, 22–23,
Fedor Selivanov, 20–21, trytrie, 21b; Thinkstock:
Dorling Kindersley, 16–17, Photos.ocm 21bl.
t=top, c=centre, b=bottom, l=left, r=right
All maps and other artwork Brown Bear Books.

Brown Bear Books have made every attempt to
contact the copyright holder.
If you have any information please contact:
licensing@brownbearbooks.co.uk

Websites
The website addresses (URLs) included in
this book were valid at the time of going to
press. However, it is possible that contents or
addresses may change following the publication
of this book. No responsibility for any such
changes can be accepted by either the author
or the publisher.

CONTENTS

ANCIENT EGYPT

One of the world's first civilisations grew up along the River Nile in Egypt from about 3100 BCE. It lasted for more than 3,000 years.

EGYPTIAN HISTORY

Egyptian history is divided into three kingdoms and two intermediate periods. The three kingdoms were the Old, Middle and New Kingdoms (see pages 28–29). These were periods when Egypt was settled and power passed peacefully from ruler to ruler. The periods between the kingdoms were less settled. New rulers seized the throne in civil wars, or foreigners invaded the kingdom. Some of Egypt's rulers came from neighbouring countries, such as Libya or Nubia. As ruling families rose and fell, different parts of the country became important. However, the lives of most Egyptians remained very stable.

A New Kingdom Egyptian family relaxes with its pets. The woman on the right is putting on makeup. A man plays a game with his son, and a slave heads for the kitchen.

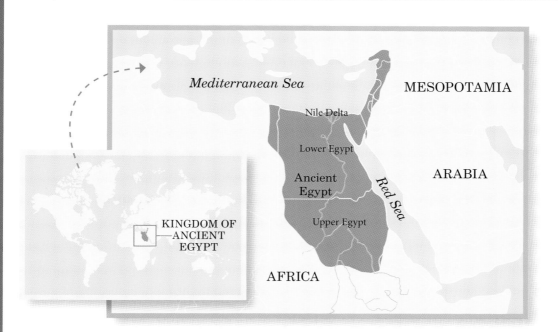

Mediterranean Sea

MESOPOTAMIA

Nile Delta

Lower Egypt

ARABIA

Ancient Egypt

Red Sea

KINGDOM OF ANCIENT EGYPT

Upper Egypt

AFRICA

ARTEFACTS

The ancient Egyptians were skilled builders, craftspeople and artists. Many of the objects they made survive today, such as temples and tomb paintings. The pyramids they built were the largest structures in the ancient world. One of the best ways to discover how the Egyptians lived and thought is by studying these artefacts. The objects enable us to step back into the world of the people who made them.

The Great Sphinx has a human head on a lion's body. The statue was carved during the Old Kingdom to guard the pyramid of King Khafre.

THE NILE

Ancient Egypt owed its existence to the River Nile. Hot, dry deserts cover more than 90 per cent of Egypt's land. The River Nile gave the ancient Egyptians food to eat and water to drink. Its regular floods allowed them to grow crops. It was also the most common way for people to travel around the country.

☞ THE FACTS

- The Nile is the world's longest river at 6,690 kilometres.
- The Nile flooded regularly once a year. The floods deposited rich, black silt on the fields along the valley.
- This soil was good for growing crops. It earned the Nile Valley its ancient nickname, the 'Black Land'. The desert was known as the 'Red Land'.

Today, Egyptians sail on the Nile in boats called feluccas, with triangular sails. In ancient Egypt, boats used sails to travel upstream and drifted downstream on the current.

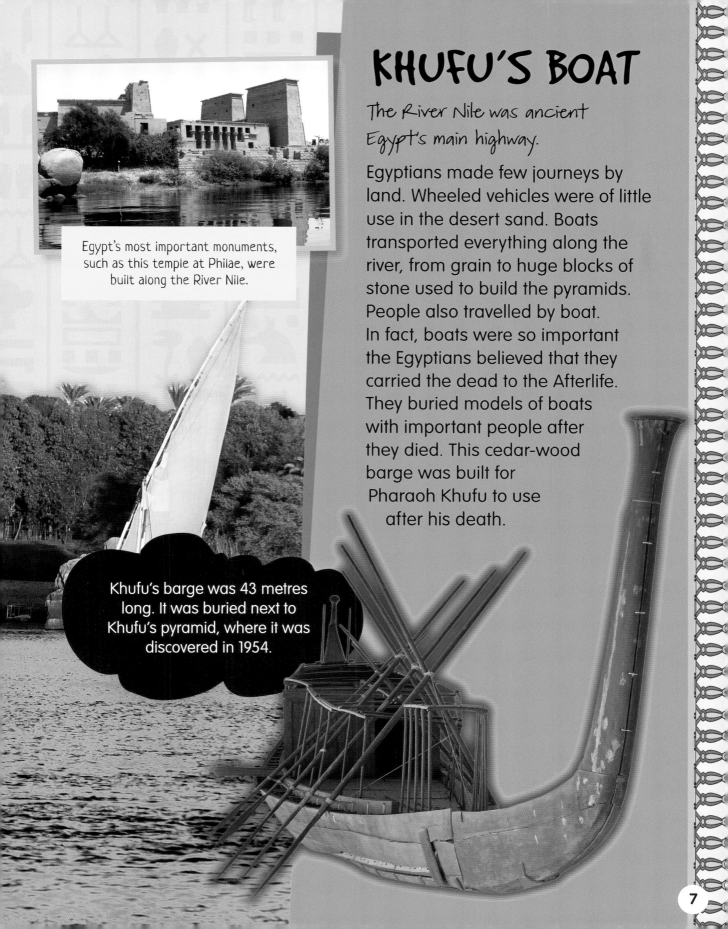

KHUFU'S BOAT

The River Nile was ancient Egypt's main highway.

Egyptians made few journeys by land. Wheeled vehicles were of little use in the desert sand. Boats transported everything along the river, from grain to huge blocks of stone used to build the pyramids. People also travelled by boat. In fact, boats were so important the Egyptians believed that they carried the dead to the Afterlife. They buried models of boats with important people after they died. This cedar-wood barge was built for Pharaoh Khufu to use after his death.

Egypt's most important monuments, such as this temple at Philae, were built along the River Nile.

Khufu's barge was 43 metres long. It was buried next to Khufu's pyramid, where it was discovered in 1954.

FARMING

The ancient Egyptians were skilled farmers. They grew more food than they needed for their families. The spare food was used to feed people in the cities and priests in the temples. The most fertile region was the flat delta where the Nile met the sea. Egyptian farmers grew grain to make bread, porridge and beer. They also raised cattle.

Workers use a shaduf to raise water from a pond to water crops. The main crops were wheat and barley. Farmers also grew flax, the fibres of which were used to weave linen.

☞ THE FACTS

- Egyptian farmers used water to irrigate their fields.
- They dug canals to transport water from the River Nile to the fields.
- Farmers used a shaduf to raise water. A shaduf was a long pole with a bucket at one end and a weight at the other. The bucket was lowered into the river. The weight made it easier to lift the bucket when it was full of water.

FRIEZE

Farming was the foundation of the ancient Egyptian civilisation.

Farmers used oxen to plough their fields. They sowed their crops of flax, wheat and barley once the Nile floods had ended during the autumn. The crops were harvested the following summer. If the Nile failed to flood, it could cause famine because there was no water to grow crops. Agriculture was so important that the Egyptians painted farming scenes inside their tombs. They believed people would continue farming in the next life.

In the Nile Delta, water channels still cut through low-lying fields.

A nobleman instructs a group of peasants. Peasants were the lowest rank of society in Egypt. They farmed, worked as labourers and helped build the pyramids.

Farmers carry stalks of wheat at a festival in a painting from the Temple of Hatshepsut, a New Kingdom ruler.

PHARAOHS

Egyptian rulers were called pharaohs. They were treated as living gods and lived in luxury. The pharaoh performed rituals to keep the other gods happy. Pharaohs passed the throne to their sons, brothers or wives. A series of pharaohs who were related to one another is a dynasty.

Seti I wears the red crown of Lower Egypt.

☞ THE FACTS

- Egypt began as two countries. Lower Egypt was based in the Nile Delta. Upper Egypt was the rest of the Nile Valley. In 3100 BCE Narmer united the two and became the first pharaoh of unified Egypt.
- The longest ruling pharaoh was Pepy II, who was on the throne for ninety-four years from 2278 to 2184 BCE.
- Women could become pharaohs. Queen Hatshepsut ruled for around twenty years.
- The last pharaoh was a woman. Cleopatra ruled from 51 to 30 BCE, when Egypt became part of the Roman Empire.

Seti I was pharaoh during the New Kingdom. This painting comes from his tomb.

GOLD MASK

The pharaoh was worshipped as the 'living Horus'. Horus (left) was the falcon-headed god of the sky.

The god Anubis welcomes Seti to the Afterlife.

This solid gold mask covered Tutankhamun's mummy inside his stone coffin, called a sarcophagus.

Tutankhamun is the most famous Egyptian pharaoh. When his tomb was discovered in 1922, it was full of treasure.

Tutankhamun died aged only 18. He may have been injured in a chariot accident. He was buried in the Valley of the Kings in Luxor with his possessions. They included a throne decorated with gold and precious stones, other pieces of furniture and statues of Anubis (see page 15) and other gods. There were even board games for the king to play.

PYRAMID BUILDERS

The most famous Egyptian artefacts are the pyramids. These huge structures were built during the Old Kingdom as tombs for pharaohs and their wives or husbands. The Egyptians built about 138 pyramids. It took skilled engineering to build them. Many no longer exist, but some have survived almost intact.

☞ THE FACTS

The first pyramid was built in about 2650 BCE by a pharaoh named Djoser. The first pyramids were built in 'steps'. Each step was smaller than the one below it. Later, architects worked out how to built pyramids with smooth sides. The first smooth-sided pyramid was built by Snefru nearly eighty years after Djoser's pyramid. Architects went on to build even larger pyramids.

Limestone blocks were brought to the site by ship then moved on rollers. Workers used stone tools to shape and smooth the stones.

GREAT PYRAMID

The largest pyramid was built at Giza for King Khufu in around 2560 BCE. It was originally 147 metres tall. Today, its top has worn away so it is a little shorter.

It took builders around twenty years to move and shape the 2.3 million blocks of stone in the pyramid. Hidden passages inside the pyramid led to a burial chamber, but explorers found no sign of Khufu or his possessions. Next to the Great Pyramid are the pyramids of his son and grandson, the pharaohs Khafre and Menkaure.

The three large pyramids at Giza are accompanied by smaller 'queens' pyramids'.

Experts believe the stones were moved up ramps of earth that were removed when the pyramid was completed.

Thousands of people worked on the Great Pyramid. Most were farmers who worked there as builders during the Nile floods.

THE GODS

The ancient Egyptians had many gods and goddesses. They believed the gods were responsible for everything in life and controlled the Afterlife. Many gods and goddesses were only worshipped in particular parts of the region. The most important gods were worshipped throughout Egypt.

☞ THE FACTS

- Osiris was the god of the dead and the Afterlife.
- The sun-god, Ra, came to be seen as the king of the gods.
- Horus was the god of the sky.
- Isis was the goddess of nature and the sky. She was seen as an ideal mother and wife.
- Thoth was the inventor of writing. He taught humans useful skills.

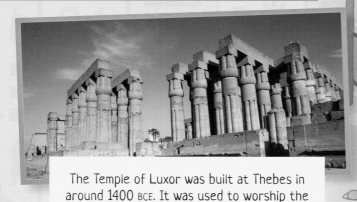

The Temple of Luxor was built at Thebes in around 1400 BCE. It was used to worship the most important gods.

The god Ra was shown with a man's body and the head of a hawk. He carried the sun disk on his head.

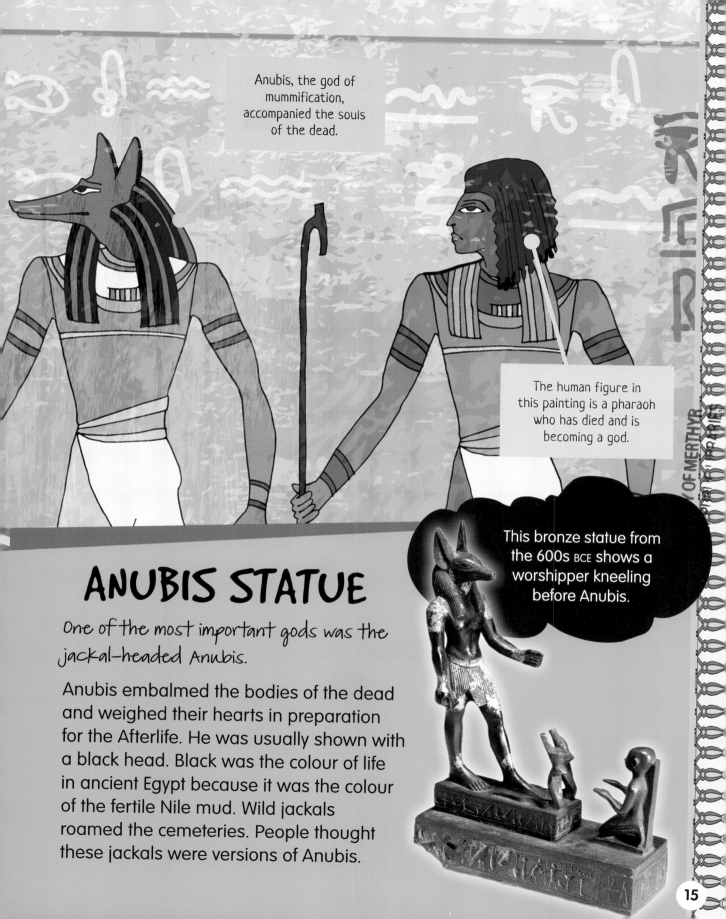

Anubis, the god of mummification, accompanied the souls of the dead.

The human figure in this painting is a pharaoh who has died and is becoming a god.

This bronze statue from the 600s BCE shows a worshipper kneeling before Anubis.

ANUBIS STATUE

One of the most important gods was the jackal-headed Anubis.

Anubis embalmed the bodies of the dead and weighed their hearts in preparation for the Afterlife. He was usually shown with a black head. Black was the colour of life in ancient Egypt because it was the colour of the fertile Nile mud. Wild jackals roamed the cemeteries. People thought these jackals were versions of Anubis.

DEATH

The ancient Egyptians believed that after people died, they were born again in the Afterlife. The dead lived there in the same way they did on Earth. The Egyptians preserved bodies so the dead could use them in the Afterlife. They buried the dead with the possessions they would need.

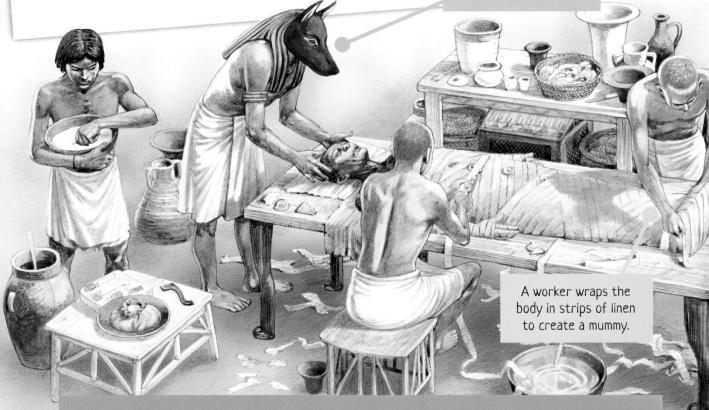

A priest wears a mask of Anubis.

A worker wraps the body in strips of linen to create a mummy.

☞ THE FACTS

- The Egyptians removed the body's internal organs. These were placed in decorated pots called canopic jars. They were buried with the body.
- The body was covered in salt to dry it. Then it was wrapped in strips of linen to make a mummy.

- The Egyptians left the heart inside the body. They believed the gods weighed the heart to see whether a person had lived a good life.
- Being made into a mummy was expensive. Many poor Egyptians were simply buried.

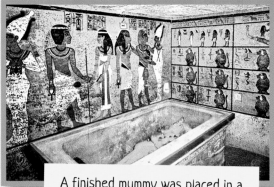

A finished mummy was placed in a coffin inside a sarcophagus.

The canopic jars had lids in the shape of the four sons of Horus. A human head protected the liver and a falcon's head the intestines. A baboon's head protected the lungs and a jackal's head guarded the stomach.

BOOK OF THE DEAD

The Egyptians believed the dead needed help to reach the Afterlife.

The dead had to make their way through an underworld called Duat. It was full of dangers, such as poisonous snakes. The insides of tombs were decorated with Books of the Dead. These were spells to protect the dead person and show them the way through Duat. In the final step of the journey, the god Anubis weighed the dead person's heart. Only if it was lighter than a feather did they reach the Afterlife.

This Book of the Dead was written on papyrus. It shows the jackal-headed Anubis weighing a heart.

A GOLDEN AGE

The New Kingdom lasted from around 1550 BCE to 1070 BCE. It was a golden age. Egypt was the strongest power in the region. Its territory expanded as it conquered its neighbours in warfare. Egyptian traders travelled to North Africa and West Asia. At home, New Kingdom pharaohs built spectacular temples. Artists, writers and mathematicians created lasting works.

☞ THE FACTS

One of the most remarkable New Kingdom rulers became pharaoh in around 1353 BCE. At first, he was known as Amenhotep IV, but he soon took the name Akhenaten. That showed his devotion to the god Aten. The pharaoh tried to make Aten the only Egyptian god. He built a new capital city dedicated to Aten, called Akhetaten. He outlawed worship of the traditional gods. However, after Akhenaten died, Akhetaten was abandoned and Egyptians went back to the old religion.

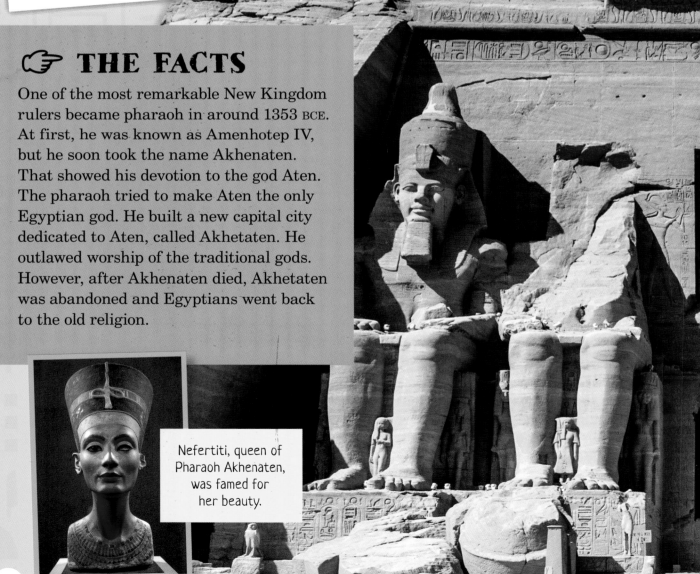

Nefertiti, queen of Pharaoh Akhenaten, was famed for her beauty.

The New Kingdom pharaoh Rameses built many monuments. His temple at Abu Simbel has four huge statues of the pharaoh. Each is over 20 metres tall.

HATSHEPSUT

Hatshepsut declared herself pharaoh in 1478 BCE. She was only the second woman known to have ruled Egypt, after Sobekneferu, three hundred years earlier.

During Hatshepsut's reign, Egypt grew richer and more powerful. Hatshepsut usually had herself shown as a male pharaoh. She built herself a huge temple that still stands near the Valley of the Kings.

This carving of Hatshepsut shows her wearing a false beard. Male pharaohs were also shown wearing false beards.

WRITING

The Egyptians had three types of writing. They used about 700 picture symbols called hieroglyphs to write on monuments. A simpler form of hieroglyphs called hieratic was used for writing important documents. For everyday documents they used an even simpler form of writing called demotic.

Hieroglyphs were carved into stone. These hieroglyphs were carved into the wall of a temple in Karnak. Hieroglyphs were also painted on the insides of tombs.

☞ THE FACTS

The Egyptians wrote on a kind of paper called papyrus made from reeds. Paper makers smashed the stalks of the reeds to separate their fibres. They mixed the fibres with water to form a thick paste. Then they spread the mixture in a thin layer to dry into sheets. Scribes sharpened the hard outer parts of the reed to make pens.

All writing was done by trained scribes. Most ordinary Egyptians could not read or write.

ROSETTA STONE

For centuries after the end of ancient Egypt, no one knew how to read hieroglyphs.

The ancient symbols were a mystery until the nineteenth century. In 1799, French soldiers in Egypt dug up an old stone at a place called Rosetta. The granite stone had three copies of the same text. The text was written in hieroglyphs, demotic and ancient Greek. Scholars at the time understood ancient Greek, so they could read this section. Over the next decades, archaeologists tried to use the Greek to decipher the hieroglyphs and demotic. The code was finally broken by a French scholar named Jean-François Champollion. He learned to read the demotic part in 1806 and the hieroglyphs in 1822.

The Rosetta Stone contains three copies of an announcement by a pharaoh named Ptolemy V. The stone was carved in 196 BCE.

Papyrus reeds grew along the banks of the River Nile.

DAILY LIFE

Egypt was the richest country in the ancient world, but most Egyptians were peasants. They farmed the land and lived in small houses made from mud bricks. The most important food was bread made from barley or wheat. The Egyptians also used barley to make a thick beer. They drank beer instead of water, because they had noticed that water from the Nile made people ill.

The village of Deir el Medina was built for workers. The people who lived there built tombs for wealthy Egyptians.

☞ THE FACTS

- There was plenty of food to go around except in times of famine.
- Pharaohs gave their people grain and people fished in the Nile.
- Boys from wealthy families went to school from the age of seven. They learned maths and writing.
- Most girls did not go to school.
- Women had the same legal status as men, which was unusual in ancient societies.
- Women could own property, inherit money and divorce their husbands.

An Egyptian couple harvest crops.

Each house had two main rooms as well as a bedroom, a kitchen and a cellar. The houses had flat roofs that acted as outdoor rooms.

BOARD GAME

The Egyptians loved to relax. They ate, drank and played games. Music was also popular.

One of the most popular ways to relax was by playing board games. The Egyptians invented some of the first games in the world. The game shown below is called senet. It has counters and a board marked with 30 squares in three rows of 10. Players threw dice to move their counters. The winner was the first person to take all his or her counters off the board. This represented successfully passing into the Afterlife. The board had a drawer underneath to store the counters and dice.

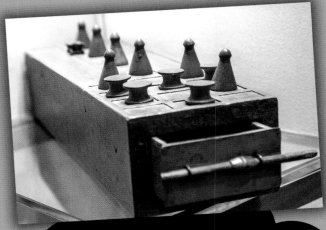

This senet game belonged to a royal architect named Kha. It was buried in his tomb, which was discovered in 1906.

FASHION

The Egyptians were one of the earliest peoples to follow fashion. Wealthy Egyptians wore clothes woven from linen so fine it was almost see-through. Ordinary Egyptians wore simple loincloths and tunics made from rough fabrics. Everyone kept themselves clean by bathing in the Nile. They used mud baths and oils to keep their skin soft.

☞ THE FACTS

- Wealthy Egyptian men and women both wore bright makeup.
- They used a black powder called kohl to draw thick lines around their eyes.
- Wealthy people put pieces of wax under their wigs. As the wax melted, it released perfume.
- Pharaoh Cleopatra bathed in donkeys' milk to keep her skin soft. She had a herd of 700 donkeys to produce the milk.
- Wealthy Egyptians were buried with anti-wrinkle cream made from spices and clay to keep them looking young in the Afterlife.

Women take part in a festival. They have used makeup to make their eyes appear large.

The last pharaoh, Cleopatra, was famed for her beauty.

PALETTE OF NARMER

In the late nineteenth century, archaeologists found a decorated stone 63.5 centimetres tall.

The stone dates from the thirty-first century BCE, when Upper and Lower Egypt were united. It is carved with designs showing Narmer, the first pharaoh of Egypt. Experts think it might have been a special version of an everyday object. One suggestion is that the palette was used to grind powder to make cosmetics. Such a special object probably belonged to a temple. The cosmetics may have been used to decorate the faces of statues of the gods.

Most people shaved their heads and wore wigs to stay cool. The wealthy wore wigs made from human hair. The poor had wigs made from straw.

The palette of Narmer was found in 1898 im a temple at a site called Nekhen. This side shows Narmer with his hand raised ready to strike a kneeling prisoner.

THE STORY OF
ISIS AND OSIRIS

Just as artefacts tell us a lot about cultures from the past, the stories people told reveal what they thought about their world. Ancient cultures used myths to explain their beliefs. The Egyptians told this myth to explain how Osiris became the god of the dead.

This tomb carving shows Osiris (left) and Isis.

The great god Ra made the world, but it was flooded until he dried up the water and made the land.

Ra was pleased with his creation, but he soon became lonely. He made himself a wife, Nut. They had many children. Ra put them to work as gods and goddesses running the world. Ra's children also had children, so soon there were even more gods and goddesses. They were all descended from Ra.

Ra loved one of his grandsons, Osiris, best of all. As a sign that Osiris was his favourite, Ra made him the first pharaoh of Egypt. That angered Osiris's brother, Set. He could not understand why Ra gave this honour to Osiris and not to him.

Osiris took the throne of Egypt. He married his great love and sister, the goddess Isis. The pair settled down to rule as the king and queen of Egypt. Soon they had a son named Horus, who was also a god.

Set grew more jealous of his brother. Eventually, he became so angry that he murdered Osiris. He chopped his brother's body into pieces, which he threw into the River Nile. Set believed this would hide his terrible crime. Soon, however, Isis heard what Set had done.

Isis was heartbroken. She searched until she had collected nearly all the pieces of Osiris. She took the pieces to the god Anubis. Although Anubis managed to put Osiris's body together again, he could not bring him back to life. When Ra heard this, he made Osiris the god of the dead, the most important job for any god or goddess. Now that Osiris was dead himself, he would be able to rule the land of the dead.

Osiris's son Horus heard about his father's murder. Although he was only a boy, he tracked down his uncle Set and killed him. Isis, meanwhile, was heartbroken. She knew she would never see Osiris again. He would dwell forever in the land of the dead, and she would live forever in the land of the living.

TIMELINE OF ANCIENT EGYPT

c.2600 BCE
The Old Kingdom of ancient Egypt begins.

c.1700 BCE
The Second Intermediate Period begins.

c.2160 BCE
The Old Kingdom ends and the First Intermediate Period begins.

c.2040 BCE
The Middle Kingdom begins.

c.3100 BCE
Upper and Lower Egypt are unified by the pharaoh Narmer.

3000 BCE

2000 BCE

1500 BCE

c.2560 BCE
The first pyramid is built at Giza.

c.2650 BCE
Pharaoh Djoser builds the first step pyramid.

c.1700 BCE
The Hyksos people invade the Nile Delta.

c.1550 BCE
The New Kingdom begins.

1070 BCE
The Third
Intermediate
Period begins.

332 BCE
The Egyptian
empire is ruled
by a Greek
dynasty.

c.1323 BCE
The pharaoh Tutankhamun dies
aged 18, having restored
traditional religion.

1400 BCE | **1250** BCE | **1000** BCE

c.1478 BCE
Hatshepsut
becomes the
second woman
to rule Egypt.

1274 BCE
Rameses II fights
the Hittites in
the Battle of
Kadesh.

30 BCE
Cleopatra dies
and Egypt
comes under
control of
the Romans.

600 BCE
The Late Period of
Egyptian history
begins.

c.1353 BCE
Akhenaten comes to
the throne. He forces
Egyptians to worship
only Aten the sun god.

GLOSSARY

Afterlife the place where the dead live after they die

allied working together to achieve a particular goal

archaeologists people who study old ruins and objects to learn about the past

architects people who design and construct buildings

artefacts things that are made by people, particularly in the past

canopic jars jars for storing the organs of the dead in a tomb

civil wars conflicts between two sides from the same country

deities gods and goddesses

delta a fan-shaped region created where a river divides into many small channels as it nears the sea

dynasty series of rulers who all come from the same family

embalmed preserved a body from decaying

famine a time of widespread and severe hunger

frieze a carved or painted horizontal band on a wall

hieroglyphs stylized pictures used as a form of writing

intermediate taking place between two periods of time

irrigate to artificially water land in order to grow crops

jackal a long-legged wild dog

linen a fine, light cloth woven from the fibres of the flax plant

minerals non-organic substances that occur naturally in Earth's crust

mummy the body of a human or animal that has been preserved and wrapped in bandages

organs separate parts of the body with specific functions, such as the heart, brain and lungs

palette a slab for mixing colours or cosmetics

pyramid a structure with a square base that tapers to a point

rituals solemn ceremonies that follow a series of actions

sacred connected with a god, and so very holy

sarcophagus a stone coffin that is often decoratively carved

scribes people who write and copy out documents

shaduf a device like a lever for moving water

silt mud deposited by a river

sphinx a creature with the body of a lion and the head of another animal or human

FURTHER RESOURCES

Books

Writing History The Ancient Egyptians, Anita Ganeri
(Franklin Watts, 2017)

History Detective Investigates Ancient Egypt, Rachel Minay
(Wayland, 2017)

The Best and Worst Jobs in Ancient Egypt, Clive Gifford
(Wayland, 2016)

History in Infographics The Ancient Egyptians, Jon Richards
(Wayland, 2016)

What They Don't Tell You About the Ancient Egyptians, David Jay
(Wayland, 2013)

Websites

www.ancientegypt.co.uk/menu.html
This is the menu page for a British Museum site about ancient Egypt,
with links to many of the museum's Egyptian treasures.

www.bbc.co.uk/education/topics/zg87xnb/resources/1
This BBC site has links to many videos about life in ancient Egypt
aimed at students.

www.bbc.co.uk/history/ancient/egyptians/
This BBC page gives an overview to all aspects of Egyptian civilisation.

www.historyforkids.net/hatshepsut.html
This site has a biography of Hatshepsut, the famous
female pharaoh of the New Kingdom.

www.primaryhomeworkhelp.co.uk/Egypt.html
This page about ancient Egypt is intended to help students
with study projects.

INDEX